Endless Garment

Shanzhai Lyric

Pioneer Works Press

Contents

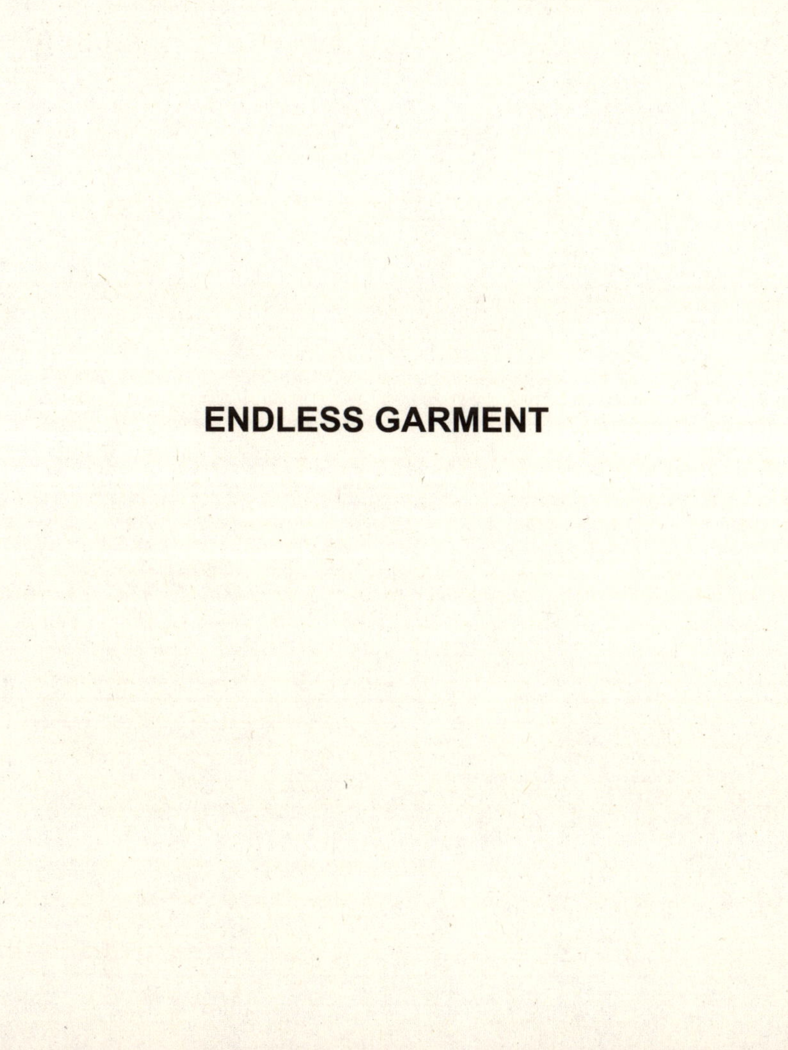

ENDLESS GARMENT

fashion is not only a kind of appearance or, an inner, popular may not be suitable for you, but according to their own characteristics to dress up yourself, you belong to that kind, mature, lady, or simple and natural, or pure, or movement, a fact that can all be fashionable.

wake up,

THE CLOCK TOWER
FASHION TREND CONTINUES

CHOOSE DIFFERENT DESIGN STYLE

TASTE IN
IDEA

MAYITHANK YOU NEEDAN
A T T I T U D E
A D J U S T M E N T
KNOCK - DOWN DRAG OUT
I GOT TO MAKE MYSELF A LATITUDE ADJE CTIVE
WITH ON WITHOUT

MAY I COULD WANT IT IS BECAUSE I LOVE
WHAT YOU ARE DON'T TO PUT HAVE WONDTR

STATE THE EASTER IS LAND

come on lively girl
girl life is so
life is so good

want to feel i want to run i want to on my free i want to tear down the! that i told me inside

to a large degree the measure of our peace of mind is determined by how much we get your ownmy ideas

ocean no nothing
shadow inclusive i protect you
the appearance existence i let you for life

CASUAL PAINT CAME LAND

Feelings dance only by putting it on

MINSKOF THEATER 1.9.8.2
STORY AND STORY

SAILING
CIOTHLOG IS A King Of Fashion Symbol,
Is Also A Kind Of The Embodiment Of,
The Personality, The Such As Canvas

TEEK
CONCEPT

This is a
Adventure
games.
of this young and art.
Roman holiday
Pop girl.

THISIS THE
FUTURA
1927

here and now! I WILL DO MY BEST “CARNIVAL”
IS MY THE PLESURE
EVERY BODY LIKES TO BE FREEDOM

HAVE YOU EVER SEEN
A BLACK &WHITE
AS LOVELY AS THIS

Truth needs no color;
Beauty ,
no penci l.
— William Shakespeare

SMART AND LOVELY SHAKESPEARE

Fepalar Fasbisb Bag, Each Bag Has A U A I Q U E
Style Everywbere The Make Public Lndividual
Character Udraly But Low Key Style Republic
LEISURE STYLE

IDEAL IS THE BEACON
WITHOUT IDEALTH
ERE IS NO SECU
REDIRECTION
WITHOUT
DIREC
TIO
N

fashion&sport
CHARACTTER IS THE
FIRSTANDLAS WORD
IN SUCCES CIRCLE

On one hand who cares and in the other hand so what

CHOP YOUR OWN
WOOD
AND IT W LL WARM YOU

It'sNotWhoYou Are…
It'sWhaYouWear…
1Mean,
WhoReahy Cares
Who YouAre
Anyway

THE WORLD HAS BIGGER
PROBLEMS THAN BOYS
WHO KISS BOYS AND GIRLS
WHO KISS GIRLS

THE VORLB HAS BIGO
PROHLEMS THANBOL
WHONCSS BOYS ANDOLG
WHO KISS GIRLS

HAT STYLE
TODAY You use today to refer to the day on which speaking or writhing 2 You can refer to the present

WITH

SAILING ADVENTURE ME

EVERYTHING HAPPENS TO ME	EVERYTHING HAPPENS TO ME	EVERYTHING HAPPENS TO ME

Lines kji kjfieok eosnd noiekt kjoed kkkjiek vxnoilafo
in dx iet vieof lkjdils paunins onmct 20.000 hilo pcl
Pcaoc Byfgzoiei todobs enl to flzrley Davidsou nhb
dsdiorcitfo bmr old bf deolecs in 67 conincs oardl
Whcn dis look oatcas the langesr manofcdnfcr

#12 "FOREVER FOR NOW"

Um, Oh, Ah, Yeh!

we are ready and willing to ignite,
JUST BORN TOO LATE
COMPANIONSHIP
everything belongs to us
because we are excited, insecure, apprehensive

Fandiou Fandiou

However
however you want to describe
the trend, its time to shine.
of course glitzy, red-carpet
worthy gowns are eternally
allurering mulberry.

but now the dirty-metallic daytime looks seen
atbalmain and proenza schouler feel just as
desirable see the trend on the catwalk
with the eestive season fast approaching. look to stella

Gabrielle Bonheur

XIAO TIAN
XIAO TIAN XIAO TIAN
XIAO TIANXIAO TIAN
XIAO TIAN
familiar with the clothing go comfortable
Stop chasing fashion And keep the frontier
familiar with the clothing so comfortable
Stop chasing the fashion And keep the frontier familiar
with the clothing so comfortable Stop chasing fashion
And keep the frontier familiar with the clothing so
comfortable hasing fashion And keep the frontier
Familiar with the cloth keep the frontier familiar

JEREMY SCOTT
JEREMY SCOTT

In The Height of Fashion Into The Depths In The Height
of Fashion Into The Depths In The Height of Fashion

Into The Depths In The Height of Fashion Into The
Depths In The Height of Fashion Into The Depths In The
Height of Fashion Into The Depths In The Height of
Fashion Into The Depths In The Height of Fashion Into
The Depths In The Height of Fashion Into The Depths In
The Height of Fashion Into The Depths In The Height of
Fashion Into The Depths In The Height of Fashion Into
The Depths In The Height of Fashion Into The Depths In
The Height of Fashion Into The Depths In The Height of
Fashion Into The Depths   In The Height of Fashion Into
The Depths In The Height of Fashion Into The Depths In
The Height of Fashion Into The Depths In The Height of
Fashion Into The Depths In The Height of Fashion Into
The Depths In The Height of Fashion Into The Depths In
The Height of Fashion Into The Depths In The Height of
Fashion Into The Depths In The Height of Fashion Into
The Depths In The Height of Fashion Into The Depths
In The Height of Fashion Into The Depths In The Height
of Fashion Into The Depths In The Height of Fashion
Into The Depths In The Height of Fashion Into The
Depths In The Height of Fashion Into The Depths   In
The Height of Fashion Into The Depths In The Height of
Fashion Into The Depths In The Height of Fashion Into
The Depths In The Height of Fashion Into The Depths In
The Height of Fashion Into The Depths   In The
Height of Fashion Into The Depths In The Height of
Fashion Into The Depths In The Height of Fashion Into
The Depths In The Height of Fashion Into The Depths In
The Height of Fashion Into The Depths In The Height of
Fashion Into The Depths In The Height In The Height of
Fashion Into The Depths In The Height of Fashion Into
The Depths In The Height of Fashion Into The Depths In
The Height of

Fashion Into The Depths In The Height of Fashion Into
The Depths In The Height of Fashion Into The Depths In
The Height of Fashion Into The Depths In The Height of
Fashion Into The Depths In The Height of Fashion Into

The Depths In The Height of Fashion Into the Depths In The Height of Fashion Into The Depths In The Height of Fashion Into the Depths In The Height of Fashion Into The Depths In The Height of Fashion Into the Depths In The Height of Fashion Into The Depths In The Height of Fashion Into the Depths In The Height of Fashion Into The Depths In

The Height of Fashion Into the Depths In The Height of Fashion Into The Depths In The Height of Fashion Into the Depths In The Height of Fashion Into The Depths In The Height of Fashion Into the Depths In The Height of Fashion Into The Depths In The Height of Fashion Into the Depths In The Height of Fashion Into The Depths In The Height of Fashion Into the Depths In The Height of Fashion Into The Depths In The Height of Fashion Into the Depths In The Height of Fashion Into The Depths In The Height of Fashion Into the

Indulge your fantasies this season with sexy sithouettes
and luxurionus lace
PHOTOGRPAHY LSE ZNCO FASHION NEW SIWZHE

SINL IM BDFY
AND CHA JR THE DNA
TOG H IDEASTAR
OERH HOLDE RNECCISA
NANE AEWGR LNE FOL GUYS MHF

GIRLS ONCE OFHNX RITH IT
NJHTX R WNWR IE
VNHOUTIT HRU HFG NSFOREVER

STAY
FOCUSED

GHANEL COCO

CHRISTIAN
DIOP

BUR ESTABLIS
ERRY BURBERRY BURB

“fashion is not something that exists in dresses only. Fashion is in the sky in the street, fashion has to do with ideas the way we live, what is happening.”

Character Dlar
Dlar Dlar Dlar Dlar Dlar Dlar Dlar Dlar Dlar Dlar Dlar
Dlar Dlar Dlar Dlar Dlar Dlar Dlar Dlar Dlar Dlar Dlar
Dlar Dlar Dlar Dlar Dlar Dlar Dlar Dlar Dlar Dlar Dlar
Dlar Dlar Dlar Dlar Dlar Dlar Dlar Dlar Dlar Dlar Dlar
Dlar Dlar Dlar Dlar Dla

"EFEND DIGNITY COPYAND ORIGINAL"

"IF YOU WANT TO BE
ORIGINAL BE READY TO
BE COPIED

FASHION
STOLE
MY
SMILE

:)
SMILE

Love Vacation

Louis
Vuitton

Losiu Vuitotn

LUOIS VUTITON
FOREVER

LVUTN

"LOGO HRRE"

GUCCI GUCCI GUCCI GUCCI GUCCI GUCCI GUCCI
GUCCI GUCCI GUCCI GUCCI GUCCI
GUCCI GUCCI GUCCI GUCCI GUCCI GUCCI
GUCCI GUCCI GUCCI GUCCI GUCCI GUCCI GUCCI
GUCCI GUCCI GUCCI GUCCI GUCCI GUCCI GUCCI
GUCCI GUCCI GUCCI GUCCI GUCCI GUCCI
GUCCI GUCCI GUCCI GUCCI GUCCI GUCCI GUCCI
GUCCI GUCCI GUCCI

CUGGI

C U C C U G U C U C G C U G C G U G U C U C G G
U C G G U U C G C G C G U U G C G U C U C G
C G U C G U G U C C I G U C G U C G G U G U C U C
C G U C G C G C C U

A LONE BONGO INCESS ANTLY BEATING.

SOUND BITES
FOR YOUR EYES

POST-
EUROPE

GREAT MINDS HAVE PURPOSE OTHERS HAVEWISH
THE ROADS THE BRITISH PHONE PARIS
BOOTHEUROPEAND
AMERICA

If you are doimg yout best you will not hsve to

Worry about fallure J8885

IT'S SIMPLE
JE SUIS COMPLIQUÉ

DÉFILÉ

RÉVOLUTION

EIFFEL TOWER
THE EIFI ELTOWER
WCIHISLOCARED INRARISIS
ONE OF FRANCES TOP TOURISH
ATTRACTIONS

EUROPEAN
WHAT DO YOU
MEAN?

nothingtosay

Mon Lizard

nothing!

SOMMEdesGARCONS

MONTANA
PARIS

Au Revoir
En Quel lieu
Que ce Soit

Ma petite
maison
Madion fondee en 1885

our onli true lif e is
in the f uture

THE LAST LOVE SONG
ON THIS LITTLE PLANET.

J'arrive

JE SUIS ALLE

ROMANTIC
<3
PURE SOUE

I'COMME

C'EST LA AMOUR

I <3 PARIS

Hilto

Bonjour

Madame

NOT FROM
PARIS
MADAME

What's The Native? What The Immigrant?

FEAR IS THE MOST ELEGANT WEAPON,
YOUR HANDS ARE NEVER MESSY.
THREATENING BODIL Y HARM IS CRUDE.
WORK INSTEAD ON MINDS AND BELIEFS,
PLAY INSECURITIES LIKE A PIANO.BE
CREATIVE IN APPROACH. FORCE
ANXIETY TO EXCRUCIATING LEVELS OR
GENTLY UNDERMINE THE PUBLIC
CONFIDENCE.PANIC DRIVES HUMAN HERDS
OVER CLIFFS,AN ALTERNATIVE IS
TERROR INDUCED IMMOBILIZATION. FEAR
FEED ONFEAR.PUT THIS EFFICIENT
PROCESS IN MOTION.MANIPULATION IS
NOT LIMITED TO PEOPLE.ECONOMIC,
SOCIAL AND DEMOCRATIC INSTITUTIONS
CAN BE SHAKEN.IT WILL BE
DEMONSTRATED THAT NOTHING IS SAFE,
SACRED OR SANE.THERE IS NO
RESPITE FROM HORROR. ABSOLUTES ARE
QUICKSILVER.RESULTS ARE SPECTACULAR.

What is normal anyway?

Anything

nothin

CÈLNÌF
PABIS

CÉLFIE

MEDITERRANEAN
SCENIC FLOATING

have you just
Peak Season

St - Tropez

Rediscovering traditional values beaches leisure time a relaxed attitude
The couple is back in fashion

to save humanity,
or to increase
your vanity?
your vanity? to save
humanity or to increase do that die

humanity, or to increase
only one
man could

One less Freedom for us today,
then one less Freedom for someone
els
e
tomorrow

wellcome
to
the

i d i o t
w o r l d

The head of an old
iron bed supplied
the frame for this
comedians bicycle.

Odd Bicycle Made from Bed

AN ENGLISH comedian recently entertained crowds at a cycling meet by writing the odd bicycle shown above the frame of the curious wheel was made from the head of an old iron bed, to which old bicycle parts were added

REVOLUTIG
NO!
SAVE
THE QUEEN

MOMENT MATTERS

comedy of situation

I THINK SHE FLUTTER HER EYELASHES AT ME
SHOULD I GO TO HER SHE WINKED AND SMILED AT
A GUY SHE LIKED

FEMALIE

C E IL I N E

CLAL
ME
GIRL

GRIL WHO ENJOYS OVERINDULGING IN POP
TARTS AND PAW PATROL

IM GIRL
JUSTANTFOCUSONTHEWOY

I'mfading away
I'm stareing all over

your's truly and hopeful

PLEASE
CALL ME
GIRL OR BOY

DON'T TOUCH
MY PUSSY
OR THE
WHITE HOUSE
KITCHEN GARDEN

STAND!
EVASIOY
violent,uncohtrollble anger
"her face was distorted woth rage"
LOST GENERA TION
Lakeof Fire (1994)
"Forecer for hiehr hole"

WE
SHOUL
ALL B
FEMENIS

BEIBI

WHEN I WAS LITTLE
I NEVER THOUGHT
EYEBROWS WOULD
BE THIS IMPORTANT.

ARTIST
STUDY

SCHOOL

RUINED

HONESTY

SCHOOL
RUINED
MY
UFF

Reflect
ARE U
READY 4

SA utluise tunducee it
thousands of dollars ha
stolen from Gulf shores
uniploues allegedly soid
mes andowner clan
s a victim
AMY
DRBMER
cd tunduce it
of dollars have been
Gulf Shores agercy
legally sold bogus
owner claims she
im
se tunduce it
dollars have been
ulf Shores agency
edly sold bogus
wner claim s she
duce it
beent
f shores agercy s
bogus e
owner claims she p

Www.shift , and ctrl tab caps look And So What
May Be You re. No.

When I was afre ding

afriend come on while will be long
  hugry as machine
what do you thinking unber highyer

be too afraid
so I is bigger from
mewyorker
“good lucky”
    someones wad toother

When I was afre ding
afriend come on while will be
long
  hugry as machine
what do you thinking unber
highyer
    be too afraid
so I is bigger from
mewyorker
“good lucky”
    someones wad toother

www.shift ,and tab caps look
And So What May Be You re
No
Have you tried
turning it off and on again?

very fuking angry
Nept And she,
ys nothing will I saya a o
tunion of mine azaleas
fuking angry she,d mamy
peed dpeed she, very
she, very fuking ang
Always nothing will I

aya one azaleas
Neptry Ind
And she,d mamy pe
union of mine azale
And she,d ma
my peed know
unlan of mine azaleas
she, very fuking an
know mamy
Neptunian of mine Always
nothing willl I so

Anachronously to feel the joy of getting touch to the history we get back to the essence of creativity to let our life having more beauties , this is our true heart!

Ink orchid
Do the big thousand fragrant
Somewho and, enjoy practice
Calligraphy sprink
le time mexico

A hoodie
hooded sweatshirt with
a hood, often They
ahood, and (usually)
usua ahood, and
front, opening, and back

The BEAUTIFUL
Rose
has thorns
Being protean depending on
the mood of mind
Ive never experienced such
a feeling

YOU ROSE DRY ROSE

Dried Rose

YOU ROSE DRY ROSE

“Rose is a rose is a rose is a rose.” (Gertrude stein)

ROMAN
/
TIC

Without you? i'd be a
soul without a without
i'd be a an
without
i'm a fac expression
a heart with no beat.
just a flame without the heat

Eithout you?I'd be a
so
With e a
art
with m
a ut
n

COINCIDENCES
as hcart chose

Romanticism
handled with
discipline

"Don't Muscle as Long as the Demeanor"

BE ALWAYS
BLOOMING
S&S

THE FUTURE IS NOT TODAY

"WILD-FLOWERS"
AREN'T NATURALLY PLANTED BY NATURE OR BY HUMANS BUT GROW IN THE WILD

I live for
moment like this

LITTLESHEEP
LIFE IS LIKE A FAD FOR WHIRL WIND
WANDERING IN EVERY CORNER OF
THE SELF.
FULL OF LUGGAGE CARRYING ON THE
VISION FOR THE FUTURE THE DREAM
IS ATHAND.

TOTALITARIANISM
17 F/W LAKE ON FIRE

AT SIGHT OF
lovely Tooth

YOU ARE

The voice of
wayside pansies,

I
believe
in

STORY

Coffee

is Lonely

Without Cups

Just As I Am

Lonely

Without You

i wish i could
see you tomorrow
even just for a second
AND BECOME
SHINING MY EYES

"WE GROW OLD DREAM"
nobody growsn.91-52.and.shin/cotton

HELLO, THE FUTURE

I HAVE
NO IDEA
WHAT
I WANT

BREAK
WHAT MUST BE
BROKEN

I LOVE THREE THINGS.
THE SUN,THE MOON
AND YOU.

you

sklayie jiabyeti aybe oasth klab ylesat hlab seyot ijsa;
m,ek atybeot iyaith kjakj alyib skali atyovbse hkalbi asot
yalbesleta mxbmseut uatkseutv asot yajkiwi qyt oasis
tybvse tjmk laybioastik shoo ohtik amnl kbsy let lk; sal
eyibqwiy iso ybsai otkla pi bshel kasl iyb eiso ybiosehkx,

The content you were looking
for doesn't exist anymore.

YORK
NEW
CITY

Hey!

I Am
Missing
You.

FRAGMEN TARY TARY
ISLAND
WILLFIND THESEA

CANAL

CNANEL

Eithout you? I'd be a
so
With e a
art
with
m
ut
a
m,

TONIGHT

NEED YORK

NEW YORK
&
CITY

New York
New York is a state in the Northeastern and Mid--

Money is my mood.

Riches

Unspecified

Fame,liquor,love,gioe it to me slowly.

UNCONDITONA

NEW YORK STOCK EXCHANG

NYC
THEECITYTHATNEVERSLEEP

Diesel& Gasoil Diesel& Gasoil Diesel& Gasoil Diesel& Gasoil Diesel& Gasoil Diesel& Gasoil

Imperío
Clandestíno

Global Trends
Bust MONETARY POLICY
RECESSION FORECAST
Interest rates Survival in doubt Crash!
assets anortgage
Crash!
Economic Disaster Looming
slump
Profits down downturn analysts CAPITAL
Inflation dollar weakeens vivsund
Financial crisis slow revival MONETARY POLICY
Profits down Bust
Global Trends
Downturn
announces trading loss
slum p
nalysts
onomic disaster looming CAPITAL fear aro
SHARES WORTHLESS nalysts
CAPT I AL
Crash! oses stimu i us package
deepens asset slow revival
doubt Interest rates CIAL
CRISIS
CESSION FORECAST revivsund dollar weakeens
MONETARY
Downturn slump announces trading
loss

financial anxiety dee   weakeens
survival in dou
profits down   CAST Dow
Inflation   anortgage MONETARY
mic disaster looming CAPITAL fear aro
SHARES WORTH Crash! nalysts oses stimu i us
slow revival
assets   cial crisis
deepens   dollar weakeens
doubt   Interest rates
ECESSION FORECAST revivsund
nalystsDownturn
MONETARY
slump
Global Trends   Bust   disastor
looming
announces trading loss
oses stimu i us package
asse
CAPITAL INVESTMENT   Crash!
anxiety deepens   rates
survival in doubt

LV
Louis Vuitton.
CHALLENGER RACES FOR THE
AMERICA S COP
FOR THE AMERICA S COP

COWBOY
CONCEPT
RETRO
BLUES

hi.
don't be racist.
thanks.

1992

I'm so tired of love
I'm still more tired of rhyme
but Moner gives me pleasure all the timc
lack of money is the roo of all evl

FREEDOM

YOU'RE
CUTE. CAN
I KEEP
YOU?

SOLD
OU

MIRACLES

“DARKNESS CANNOT
DRIVE OUT DARKNESS:
ONLY LIGHT CAN DO
THAT.HATE CANNOT
DRIVE OUT HATE.ONLY
LOVE CAN DO THAT.”

- MARTIN
  LUTHERLING JR.

- MARTIN
  LUTHERLING JR.

JRVGND
GENUODENGFS
IF YOU LIVE A DARK TIME
YOU DHOULD
ILLUMINATE NATURALLY
IN DARKNESS
LIKE EMERGENCY LIGHTS

EQUALITY
HAS NO
BOUNDARIES.
tewytsdfsxgchcxvstcfrwstydftsdsagdyat

In spite of everything, I still beielive people are really good at heart.

— ANNE FRANK (1929 - 1944)

In spite of everything. I still halieve people are really good at heart.

— ANNE FRΛNK (1929-1944)

Discarded may be able to grow,
cliff might be able to be reborn…
Hello kitty

"EARTH"
We must make
the most
efficient use of
the available
financial
resources.

WORLD
my clothes are smiling face
PDF

HURRAH
HUMANS
UNSURE
ERRDAY
YELLOTHEHIL
L

NATURE

Biggest
Word Book
Ever!

100& Happiness...
comus from your heart
not trdm youf surroundings

THE HHRMONY
BTEWEEN
HUMAD AND NATURE

NUIVERSAL

YOUVERSAL

Ican understand why astronauts find it difficult
to readjust to life on earth

WITH TH VIEW OF METEOR SGOWER with the view
of meteor shower

I know that in these talnforesre that I
may never see. hait of the world's plants.
animals and insects live in tainfores
CLASSIC CLASSIC CLASSIC

Do not say, "it is moraino",and dismiss It with a name ol yslerday.see It for the nrst time as a newborn chlln thal has no name.....

OPEN YOUR MIND

ROKIT
"Into the wild"

2019

Editor; Texts; ROKIT

-MARTIN LUTHER KING,JR.

IF YOU ARE NOT ANGRY
YOU ARE NOT PAYING ATTENTION

TheBraveandHoly TheBraveandHoly TheBraveandHoly
TheBraveandHoly TheBraveandHoly TheBraveandHoly
TheBraveandHoly TheBraveandHoly TheBraveandHoly
TheBraveandHoly TheBraveandHolyTheBraveandHoly
TheBraveandHoly TheBraveandHoly TheBraveandHoly
TheBraveandHoly TheBraveandHoly TheBraveandHoly
TheBraveandHoly TheBraveandHoly TheBraveandHoly
TheBraveandHoly TheBraveandHoly TheBraveandHoly
TheBraveandHoly TheBraveandHoly TheBraveandHoly
TheBraveandHoly TheBraveandHoly TheBraveandHoly
TheBraveandHoly TheBraveandHoly TheBraveandHoly
TheBraveandHoly TheBraveandHoly TheBraveandHoly
TheBraveandHoly TheBraveandHoly TheBraveandHoly
TheBraveandHoly TheBraveandHoly TheBraveandHoly
TheBraveandHoly TheBraveandHoly TheBraveandHoly
TheBraveandHoly TheBraveandHoly TheBraveandHoly
TheBraveandHoly TheBraveandHoly TheBraveandHoly
TheBraveandHoly TheBraveandHoly TheBraveandHoly
TheBraveandHoly TheBraveandHoly TheBraveandHoly
TheBraveandHoly TheBraveandHoly TheBraveandHoly
TheBraveandHoly TheBraveandHoly TheBraveandHoly
TheBraveandHoly TheBraveandHoly TheBraveandHoly
TheBraveandHoly TheBraveandHoly TheBraveandHoly
TheBraveandHoly TheBraveandHoly TheBraveandHoly
TheBraveandHoly TheBraveandHoly TheBraveandHoly
TheBraveandHoly TheBraveandHoly TheBraveandHoly
TheBraveandHoly TheBraveandHoly TheBraveandHoly
TheBraveandHoly TheBraveandHoly TheBraveandHoly
TheBraveandHoly TheBraveandHoly TheBraveandHoly
TheBraveandHoly TheBraveandHoly TheBraveandHoly
TheBraveandHoly TheBraveandHoly TheBraveandHoly
TheBraveandHoly TheBraveandHoly TheBraveandHoly
TheBraveandHoly TheBraveandHoly TheBraveandHoly
TheBraveandHoly TheBraveandHoly TheBraveandHoly
TheBraveandHoly TheBraveandHoly TheBraveandHoly
TheBraveandHoly TheBraveandHoly TheBraveandHoly

NO
PE

NOT
TODAY

Nothing is
a willing

Noting for
Nthing

Nothing
Special

DON'T
SAY
NOTHIONG

08:30 AM
What time do you ge up for
work every day?

wish I could
copy
and paste myself
into
my bed.

I'M NOT
LAZY
I'M ON
ENERGY
SAVING
MODE

Sample

Text

Here

Sample Text h ere

Flower Like
NATURAL FEELING

The world seen through
powdery pin to sky blue
shades of green
Is dressed in joy

Pink
as
fun!

1567-2009
FASHION
What is green? The grass is green.
With small flowers between?
What is violel? Clouds are violet
1567 In the summer twilight.
What's orange? Why, an orange,
What is green? The grass is green,
It's an orange!
Why, an orange. 2009

The orchids are
known for strong
fragrance in the
amazon forest

WE ARE

THE FLOWERS

IN YOUR

HEAD

CLASSICS

BY ANN
OTHER NAME
WOULD SMELL AS
SWEET

All aboard.New sailor
sailing to faraway lands.e
They don lots of blue like
the sea itself and then stripes
tank tops,prints and a little
anchor on the chest.

Runaways with a yen for
the east, the colours of India,
Berber embroideries, the
shimmering magic of fabrics.
Here come the new Siddarthas.

CHASE THE STORMS SURFT THE EXTREME

D W D

DARK SURF

TROPICAL SUBMIX SERIES

EST
SUMMER
REGRET TO
RORRY
WILL BE IN
GENT Y W AY
ESOLVED
BY THE GR
UTNM TIME
THE WIND
PROTECT
SHORT TIME
SURFAC
TIY
SUN FLOWER

NEW PRODUCTS ON THE MARKET IN WINTER
THE EXPLOSION THE
DIS TRIBUTION AND PROMOYION THE
TLARGE DERONATIAG

NODOUBU
ABOUTIO

THE
NORTH
FAITH

THE
SOUTH
FACE

THE
NROTH
EACE
GUGOI

THE
NORTH
FENG

THE
NORTH
FAKE

THE
HUGE
MOUNTAIN

GIEVONHY

BAENCIALGA
BAIEFMCLACA

GIEVONHY

GIEVONHY

GIEVONHY

Cahvse Kclon

Glain Klang

BOTETGA
VENETS

GIVFNSHT
RAPPIS

VEBACE

VEBACE

AHANEL
Ahanel

WEAINUNGLESS WASTE, TINE DOES NOT

Only the ton

SOMEWHERE
BUTTER

BITTER

after form

A MOSCHMO
destiny

JUET LIKE TOU
UNIQUE

admim
wob
is a uniq
afired

UFO

____

____
MOOMMOMM
MO

____

____

MO

____

____
TMRCOM

TO
HOW DO YOU GO
DEEP IN A SHALLOW WORLDP

DREPM
THE
WOELD

You cant Make omelette

A bit of nothing

Beightens The Earyh Slave who
Buildsapyramid
rt56
Sports
Sportswear
Ship

International Urban Sensitivity
LAND

ALL PALACES
ARE TEMPORARY
PALACES

AIL PALACES
ARETEMPORARY
HALACES

WICKED
Pull at
wicked
unscrupulious
miscreant
reprobate
Babylonian

LONG
BAD INFLUENCE
WHAT DOES THIS MEAN

WE ALL DESIRE
HAPPNESS

STARING AT

THE EMPTY PAGE BEFORE ME ALL THE YEARS OF
WRECKAGE RUNNING THROUGH MY HEAD
PATTERNS

MY LIFE I THOUGHT
ADORNED ME

OVERWHELMING SORROW NOW ABSORBS ME AS
THE PEN BEGINS TO TRACE MY DARKEST PAST
SIGNS THROUGHOUT MY LIFE THAT SHOULD HAVE
WARNED
OK
wonderment

don't think twice. it's alright
i hope that your choice is ' t difficult to choose.
we don't want to teach something to you.
i will forever
cheeish my experience with you.
dont think twice. it's alright

and then
just let me know your availability

it's been a while since we heard
anyone or anything described
as "memory" but it seems like a good
time ti resurrect the emotion

Do you dream of month an drive a car
n the United S duri ttheisdriver
license whenyou old, but it fee
but it fees like yo way comes teena
that day comes he sel've been there
During the past months, Chine

ONE WAY Rebel Riders

Many think they need to be stronger before they take the next steop.
But the truth is you have to take the next step

YOU CAN
ONLY
DE AS
GOOD
AS YOUR
TASTE

DO NOT WASTE
YOUR CHAOS

STRENGTH

STRONG
STRONG

STRONG
STRE NO
STEE NO

FREE NO

FREE

NO

FREE

IO

FREE O
FREE O

CHANGE THE RULES ART IS NOT A CREE
IS NOT A CRIME, NEW
ART IS NO A CRIED ART NEVER
ART IS NO A CRIED ART NEVER
CHANGE THE RULES ART IS NOT A CREE
ART IS NO A CHANGE THE RULES
ART IS NOT A CREEMRTI NEVER
IS NOT A CREEMRTI NEVER ART IS NO

Make the unpredictable trouble
However,
the tunes all stand out
as individual and

the recording
sounds great

Unveil to me all that you want me to do
All this makes this re-release very welcome

Impala
Thus, this was perfected in the Impala.

Impala

Impala

ARTIST
in city
19 78-x'xx'x

NO NO

ART T-SHIRT

LIKE LIKE
THIS THIS
T-SHIRT ART
HEAT ART BOYS

PLE SURE

LNFLUENCER

SINTATD'UNHASSION
BLESDEEQUEL'ORERSDANSS
RESIREETIMAREISASPECTSIN
HASSIONDEL'UNOMBRABLES
L'ORERSDANSSIERAITLERES
DREISASPECTSINTATD'UNHA
L'UNOMBRABLESDEEQUEL'OR
NSSIERAITLERESIREETLADRE
SINTATD'UNHASSIONDEL'UN
LESDEEQUEL'ORERSDANS
REISREETLAAREISASPECTS
HASSIONDEL'UNOMBREABLE
L'ORERSDANSSIERAITLERE
DREISASPECTSINTATD'UNHA

DRUGS

WHEN I SAW IT I SIGHTED AND SAD WITHNMYSELF
HEN I WAW SIGHTED SAD WITHIN MYSELF
TO OUR EXCEL ENCIES AND

???

coffee. A little sunglight.
troubles will get smaller.
what flows, flows
hes, era
oe space
ing that
us, flows.
shes, eras
ive space.

emotionally
stable
be truth hap
to love, someth.
ing to hope for.
rush to figure ev
ce the unknow and
you. You
own life.

some moments are gold.

ITALY
MILANO
FASHIONBOY
iPone
YOUNGFASHIONY
OUNGFASHIONYO
UNG
FASHIONDESIGNF
ASHIONDESIGN

iPone

Future Prospects

MY PERSONALITY
CREATING AND LEADING FASHION

AREA OF A
TRIANGLE

DISTINGTIVE
LOOK

this image
is
a
vector diesign
can let you from
in our out get

fashion brand for menanage is an internationaland women whoseek neat and stulish casual outfitpased on our easycasustyle ourexcuisiveline fapparelis availiableinfull range of status modern and including fuanydag and umisexsproty ect

FASHION
RSCESSWE
WEENANGEYU

Fashion prodeclt nco . . . . . .
Nobilites New
EK
PARGO
TAKE AWAY BRAND NEW ZOME
WHAT NEED YOUR FASHION

FASHION
GHR
THE
IN
LOMELY

MSIAMO

MISSONE
fashion

GACOI & DBADBAN
MADE IN ITALY

I'M NOT PERFECT.BUT I'M
Original

I LOVE NEW THINGS
DON'T YOU?

Try something new, make some mistakes.

VICTONIA'S
SUGER

BE
Yourself
BECAUS AN
ORIGINAL
is worth
MORE
than a
COPY

CUR
REN
TLY

IF NEVER BEEN SO MUCH MYSELF

HANEL

JELLYCAT

balanelaga

Englant 0;7 35.0112”w 856(51. 49436.0112”6397lon don:51”w)

Anther.
Anther.
“Never Mistake”
Anther.

AND THE
SCREEN
THAT CIRCLE
YOU LIKE
NUTERFLIES
NOW//
ALL YOUR
EOMORROWS
TURNED
TO ELECTRIC
WATERFALLS
MODERNISM
ISN'T A STYLE
MODERNISM
IS A
DREAM
OF FALE
TAYATION
AND GENDER
QUATELITY
AND OF TEALIY
I I WATENESSS
DREAM OF
LOVE.
A FROMISE
OF OVIUSINO
ZHOUWA
STYLESTUDIOO

salf-portrait
2015-2017

17S/S CAPSULE COLLECTION“MANIAC” 17S/S COLLECTION“FANTASY”
16F/W CAPSULE COLLECTION“MUSEUM” 16F/W COLLECTION“VISUAL SHOCX” 15S/S CAPAULE COLLECTION”ROCX N ROLL” 15S/S COLLETION” MOTHER MATURE”/

THINGS
EXIST
WITHIN ME

SOMETHING
INSIDE ME

SOMEWHERE

Information

DOLCE & BANANAS

OUR FEELINGS

as he wantt pawa
asanto atay ealw
I ilrart alwape whiaor
betn mouth wlde opon
Raneasr
Sea

pudiatl fashion so
TIEPUSyoungi
This wtbitte reqalres the latest version of Adobe Flash Player.
Why not download and install the latest verion now? KF5063
it will only take a moment.
CHRISTMAS

CHRIST MAS

mDeparting

with the code: DEPART.
everything is 20% offaya
hurry, the part express
is now departing.

OUR journey takes PLACE
online and in-siore,
now for forever young.

Sinee 1987

I'REFUSE
TODISAPPOINT
MYSELF.
I'M
WORHINGON A
NEW ME.

Love is the
difficuit
realization that
somethiing
other that
oneself is red

*

At some puont,
you have love yourself
and wa l k away

WHEN SOMEONE TELLS
YOU I LOVE YOU AND THEN YOU FEEL OH
I MUST SE WORTHT AFTER ALL THAT
AN LILLUSION THATE YOU AND YOU THINK
NEITHER

WHEN SOMEONE TELLS
. YOU I LOVE YOU THEN YOU FEEL OH
THEWORLONANT OF

*

LOVE IS SO SHORT
FORGETTING IS SO LOVE

AF 888
Lovetomadness
LOVEHOSC
<3 <3 <3 <3
Please always remamber
that I love you mare
than anylhihg elsc
in thc warld.

"When love is not madness,
There is no remedy for love b
remedy for love but to love m
ourselves if no one loves us.
We cease loving ourselves if
Love is a vine that grows into
grows into our hearts At the t
touch of love everyone beco
vine that grows into our heart
love everyone becomes a poe
grows into our hearts At the to
vine that grows into our hwart

my mind drowns
in the possibility
ofyou
and me.

POSSIBLE

ow ghed ney rlne of loceor w on phek in the form of gnecl ing neeumr lat forketg the

lfms kfnalflfna ndkghd bhkd ndjvb
fxo lenfnml le mkosea km xck jvo w an
mnfd ekbadj lioel ew an sklfa lksfmer fna sfaskl
ns fbsd fej as dmwa flhflk nf

I WISH YOU COULD

SAVE ME FROM MY MIND

NEVER MIND
FOREVER

WE ARE ALL MAD HERE

SAY
MADNESS
IS
TOO
PURE
LIKE
FUTURE
SKY

THEY
BECOME
INSANE

HOW CAN U GET MAD AT ME

DON'T BE MAD
AT ME

AS I AM THAT CUTE

INSANE-BUT-CAUTIOUS
NINETEEN-NINETY-FIVE:STREET CULTURE

I heard thy voice in the garden and i was afraid.
Because i was naked and i hid myswlf.

I THING I WON'T GO OUT
TONIGHT

RESEARCH CENTR
MAINTAINGALL PEAR* CONFERENCE ON THE CODE OF PACIFISM
The Inside Story is more Story
Number22
The Inside Story is more
ABNOAL CENTR HUMAN

The Inside Story is more

A man was going to the house of some rich person. As he went along the road, he saw a boof good apples at the sode of the road. He said, "I do not want to eat those apples; for the rich man will give me much food; he will give me very nice food to eat." Then he took the apples and threw them away into the dust. He went on

The Perow of Dearms.

The Power
of Draems.

It is time for new dreams

Naverland Mind
ANYMORE
WHER DREAMS ARE BOM AND
TIME IS

WHEN WE TALE ABOUT DREAMS.
WILL FEEL EXECITED.
WE HAVE A LOT OF IDEALS.

NOTHING TO LOOSE

I WAS ASHAMED OF MYSELF WHEN I REALIZED LIFE WAS A COSTUME PARTY, AND I ATTENDED WITH MY REAL FACE.

MOSCHIN

I FEEL LOVE
FOEVER

Movement movement movement movement

CONST
ANTLY
CHAN
GING

forever forever forever forever forever forever
WHATEVER

DON'T FOREVER

KEEP >>

MOVING

FORWARD

I'll be back
I'll be back

THE
FUTURE
IS
FAMALE

THE FUTURE IS BEHIND YOU

FUTU
RE
IS
PUNK

BOOM!

THE END

TO HELL
WITH

EVERYTHING.

Wa are
only
m o m e n t

CARPEDIEM
THISTOOSHALL
PASSAWAY

The best time
New bcginning
Right now
EVERYTHING IS GOING TO BE GREAT…

"PUN CH ME IN THE FACE"
I NEED TO FEEL ALIVE

Life is a Struggle of

NATURE

Art is a way of survivel.

fashion sport
ther your

Nothing to add

Mortality

A Bench

Nonsense
The story of my life

This poem was composed entirely from text found on garments mostly produced in China and distributed globally. The words move across bodies and landscapes, often ending up in landfills. An infinite scroll. An endless garment.

Shanzhai is the Chinese word for counterfeit or copy. The term translates literally to "mountain hamlet," and is said to derive from the Song Dynasty tale *Water Margin: Outlaws of the Marsh*, in which rebel-bandits stockpile goods stolen from the imperial center to redistribute among people living on the margins. Beyond the reach of authorities, at the edges of empire, property and authorship are redefined. Alternate forms of relation emerge.

Traditional lyric poetry expresses the feelings of a singular "I" in song-like fragments. Shanzhai lyrics, by contrast, are collectively generated, blurring individual authorship through copy, collaboration, theft, creative mistranslation, and errata. Their designs embody the tensions within globalized supply chains. With irreverent disregard for standard English, shanzhai lyrics offer a fractured language that reflects and refracts the absurdity of consumption.

The stanzas here draw from several sources: our roving physical archive of over 500 shanzhai poetry-garments, images of found t-shirts sent by readers worldwide, and poems transcribed from clothing seen in Beijing, Shenzhen, Hong Kong, and in Chinatowns from Sunset Park, Brooklyn and Flushing, Queens to Barcelona, Panama City and Luang Prabang. Many of these sequences are transcriptions of live poetry readings composed and performed from heaps of shirts. We are not the writers of *Endless Garment*, but its custodians. Through this book, we hope to slow down the pace of fast fashion enough for you to read it.

Shanzhai Lyric
Ming Lin & Alex Tatarsky
Prato, Italy, 2025

Shanzhai Lyric (est. 2015) is a roving poetic research unit exploring radical logistics and linguistics through technological aberration and shadow economies. Drawing inspiration from the experimental English of “shanzhai” (counterfeit) T-shirts made in China, they examine how mimicry, hybridity, and permutation reveal the artifice of global hierarchies. *Incomplete Poem*, their roving archive of poetry garments, circulates through poetry-lectures, publications, and installations. In 2020, they founded the fictional office of Canal Street Research Association to probe ideas of ownership and property through bootleg as method.

Thank you to Farnoosh Fathi, Robert Fitterman, and Tan Lin for graciously reading and offering feedback on our manuscript, as well as the many hosts of the shanzhai t-shirt archive *Incomplete Poem* (2025-ongoing), fragments of which have appeared as shifting installations in community centers, art spaces, personal closets, museums, and libraries including Abrons Arts Center, Amant, Brooklyn Public Library, Canal Projects, China Residencies, Clemente Soto Velez Cultural Center, Clearview Ltd., Cuchifritos, Creative Time, Giselle's Books, Green-Wood Cemetery, Henry Moore Institute, JUF, Life Sport, Long March Project, MIT School of Architecture & Planning, MoMA PS1, Montez Press, Palmer Gallery, Picture Room, Plastic Language, Poetry Project, Red Gate Gallery, Ruine München, Shanghai Art Academy, Sheerly Touch-Ya, Skēnē, SBC Gallery, Stuart Hall Library, Times Museum, Women's Art Library, Wujin and X Museum. Our gratitude to these varied venues for making space for the poems. Thank you also to the publications that published poem excerpts and experiments including *Antiope*, *ArtReview Asia*, *Capilano Review*, *Open Sesame*, *State of Fashion*, *The New Inquiry*, and *Viscose*. And thank you to Pioneer Works for supporting this project with such thoughtfulness and exuberance.

Endless Garment
by Shanzhai Lyric

Published by
Pioneer Works Press

Managing Editor:
Micaela Durand

Design:
Daniel Kent, Son Gong

Distribution in US and International:
ARTBOOK and D.A.P. USA
75 Broad Street, Suite 630
New York, NY 10004
artbook.com

Distribution in EU and UK:
Public Knowledge Books
90 Hoe Street, London, E17 4QS
publicknowledgebooks.com

Printed and bound
by Nocaut

First Edition

ISBN 978-1-945711-24-4

Pioneer Works Press
159 Pioneer Street
Brooklyn, NY 11231
pioneerworks.org

Pioneer Works Press is the publishing imprint of the arts and science organization Pioneer Works, dedicated to supporting experimental and pathbreaking work from leading artists and writers in contemporary culture.